We Read
PHONICS™

Help the Planet

TREASURE BAY

Parent's Introduction

Welcome to We Read Phonics! This series is designed to help you assist your child in reading. Each book includes a story, as well as some simple word games to play with your child. The games focus on the phonics skills and sight words your child will use in reading the story.

Here are some recommendations for using this book with your child:

1 Word Play

There are word games both before and after the story. Make these games fun and playful. If your child becomes bored or frustrated, play a different game or take a break.

Many of the games require printed materials (for example, sight word cards). You can print free game materials from your computer by going online to **WeReadPhonics.com** and clicking on the link to "Select titles to View & Print: Game Materials." However, game materials can also be easily made with paper and a marker—and making them with your child can be a great learning activity.

② Read the Story

After some word play, read the story aloud to your child—or read the story together, by reading aloud at the same time or by taking turns. As you and your child read, move your finger under the words.

Next, have your child read the entire story to you while you follow along with your finger under the words. If there is some difficulty with a word, either help your child to sound it out or wait about five seconds and then say the word.

③ Discuss and Read Again

After reading the story, talk about it with your child. Ask questions like, "What happened in the story?" and "What was the best part?" It will be helpful for your child to read this story to you several times. Another great way for your child to practice is by reading the book to a younger sibling, a pet, or even a stuffed animal!

LEVEL 8 Level 8 introduces the letter combinations "kn" (as in *knot*), "wr" (as in *write*), "mb" (as in *comb*), and "ph" (as in *phonics*), long vowel sounds followed by "r" (as in *hear*), and "-le" endings (as in *apple*).

Help the Planet

A We Read Phonics Book: Level 8
Guided Reading: Level H

Text Copyright © 2024 Treasure Bay, Inc.

Reading Consultants: Bruce Johnson, M.Ed.

We Read Phonics™ is a trademark of Treasure Bay, Inc.

All rights reserved

Published by
Treasure Bay, Inc.
PO Box 519
Roseville, CA 95661 USA

Printed in China

Library of Congress Catalog Card Number: 2023910617

ISBN: 978-1-60115-458-3

Visit us online at:
WeReadPhonics.com

PR-11-23

Help the Planet

By Bruce Johnson

Phonics Game

Moving Up

Taking a careful look at the words in the story will help your child to reread those words or patterns another time or in another story.

Materials:
Option 1—Fast and Easy: To print free game materials from your computer, go online to WeReadPhonics.com and click on "Select Titles to **View and Print: Game Materials**." Then go to this book title and print the game materials.

Option 2—Make Your Own: You'll need 20 index cards, markers, scissors, and paper clips. Write each of the following 10 words on two index cards to make two sets of cards: **planet, helping, fear, years, nearby, dear, simple, bottle, example**, and **little**.

1. Take one set of the cards and cut up the letters, but keep letter combinations together. For example, cut *planet* into three cards: "**pl**," "**an**," and "**et**." Cut the rest of the words as follows: **h/el/p/ing, f/ear, y/ear/s, n/ear/by, d/ear, s/im/ple, b/ot/tle, ex/am/ple,** and **l/it/tle**.

2. Place a card that is not cut up on the table, and the matching card with cut up letters in order about six inches below.

3. The child first reads the top word. She then slowly repeats the first sound while sliding the matching letter underneath the top letter. Continue with the remaining letters and sounds. Finish by rereading the word again.

4. To add a little bit of fun, create some nonsense words. After creating a real word, switch some of the consonants around to make some nonsense or silly words. Reread the words.

5. Paper clip the complete word to the matching cut up letters to keep for another time.

Sight Word Game

Go Fish

Play this game to practice sight words used in the story.

Materials:
Option 1—Fast and Easy: To print free game materials from your computer, go online to WeReadPhonics.com and click on "Select Titles to **View and Print: Game Materials**." Then go to this book title and print the game materials.

Option 2—Make Your Own: You'll need 18 index cards and a marker. Write each word listed on the right on two cards. You will now have two sets of cards.

1. Using one set of cards, ask your child to repeat each word after you. Mix the cards together, and deal three cards to each player. Players don't let others see their cards. Put the remaining cards face down in a pile.

2. Player 1 asks player 2 for a particular word. If player 2 has the word card, then he passes it to player 1. If player 2 does not have the word card, then he says, "Go Fish," and player 1 takes a card from the pile. Player 2 takes a turn.

3. Whenever a player has two cards with the same word, he puts those cards down on the table and says the word out loud. The player with the most matches wins the game.

4. Keep the cards and combine them with other sight word cards you make. Use them all to play this game or play sight words games featured in other **We Read Phonics** books.

about

again

before

every

little

live

many

maybe

water

The planet we live on is our only home.
It is up to us to help take care of it.

That may seem hard but do not fear. There are many simple things you can do to help.

Too much trash is not good for the planet.
Think before you throw something away.

Could you use it again? Is it possible to use it in a new way?

Can you write on both sides of paper? Maybe you can turn your paper over to use the other side. You could write a paragraph about helping the planet!

Some food comes in glass jars. Use the jars for storing items when the food is gone. You could store pens or rubber bands.

Too much plastic trash is bad for the planet. Try getting a water bottle you can use again and again.

Use a lunch box to take your lunch to school. You can use it every day.

If something is broken, think before you throw it away. Can you fix it?

Take good care of *all* your things. They could last for many years.

This could help you save money too.

Using too much power and water is not good for the planet. Use what you need—but need what you use.

For example, use lights when you need them. Turn them off when you leave the room.

Do you live far from school? Use less gas by sharing a car ride with friends. Is school nearby? Maybe you can ride your bike or walk.

A heater uses a lot of power in the winter. To stay warm, you can cuddle up with a blanket.

Keep the heat inside your house. All the windows and doors should be closed.

Games that plug in are fun, but other things are fun too. You can play checkers or kick a ball. Or make something amazing!

A sink that drips will use a lot of water. A plumber may need a wrench to stop the drip.

Running water while brushing your teeth is wrong! Turn the water off while you brush.

Growing your own food is good for the planet. If you have a yard, plant a little garden. Your mother, father, or friend can help you.

No yard? You can still have a garden. Beans and peppers can grow in a window box.

There are more things to do. You do not have to do every single one. Start with a few. Before long, you will make a real impact.

It feels good to help take care of our dear planet.

Codes

Playing with letters is a wonderful way to reinforce letters and sounds.

1. On a sheet of paper, write these "words" in code, leaving room underneath each one for your child to write the decoded word:

   okzmds, ozodq, onvdq, edzq, cdzq, khsskd, ansskd

2. Your child can "break the code" by rewriting the words using the next letter in the alphabet. For example, the letter "d" becomes the letter "e." The letter "z" is used for the letter "a." If necessary, copy the alphabet on the top of the paper.

3. Answers are *planet*, *paper*, *power*, *fear*, *dear*, *little*, and *bottle*.

4. For more word play, try to write a sentence from the story in code, changing each letter to the next letter in the alphabet.

Phonics Game

Guess the Word

This is a fun way to practice blending letter sounds together, which helps children learn to read new words.

1. Choose a simple word in the story that can be sounded out. Say the sound for each letter or letter combination in the word. For example, for the word *plastic*, say the sounds for the letters "pl," "as," "t," and "ic," with a slight pause between the sounds.
2. Ask your child to guess or say the word.
3. If your child does not reply correctly, then repeat and extend the sounds. If your child continues to have difficulty, run the sounds closer and closer together.
4. Continue with additional words from the story, such as *food*, *lunch box*, *power*, *lights*, *blanket*, *heat*, *windows*, *water*, *garden*, and *window box*.
5. For variation, let your child provide the prompt sounds to you.

If you liked *Help the Planet*,
here is another **We Read Phonics** book you are sure to enjoy!

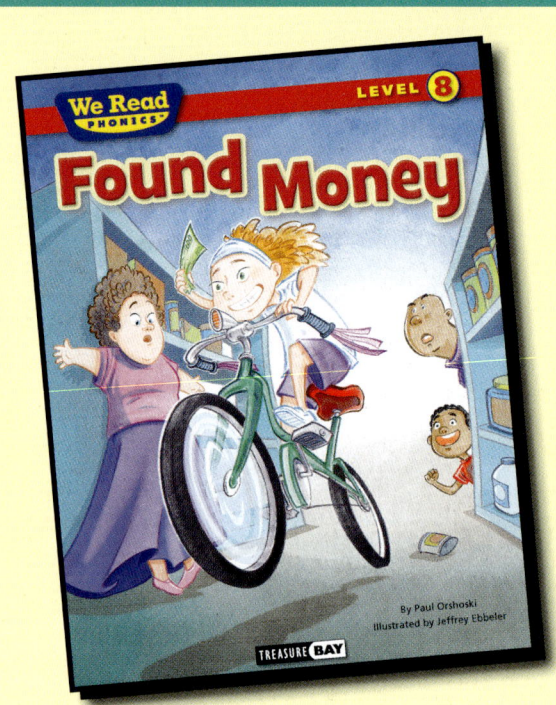

Found Money

A girl sees a new bike in a store window and thinks it is the best thing she has ever seen. When she finds a $100 bill floating through the air, she is very excited that she now has the money to buy the bike. But what will she do if she finds out who lost the $100 bill?